THIS JOURNAL BELONGS TO

Made in the USA
Columbia, SC
07 December 2024

48640266R00067